THE WIMSEY FAMILY

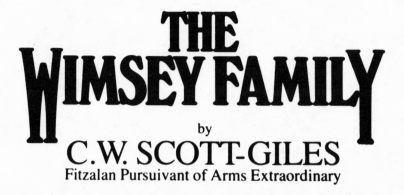

THE WIMSEY FAMILY

by

C.W. SCOTT-GILES

Fitzalan Pursuivant of Arms Extraordinary

AVON
PUBLISHERS OF BARD, CAMELOT AND DISCUS BOOKS

AVON BOOKS
A division of
The Hearst Corporation
959 Eighth Avenue
New York, New York 10019

First Avon Printing, September, 1979

AVON TRADEMARK REG. U.S. PAT. OFF. AND IN
OTHER COUNTRIES, MARCA REGISTRADA, HECHO EN
U.S.A.

Printed in the U.S.A.

Avon Books by
Dorothy L. Sayers

Garter stall-plate of Gerald de Wimsey, 5th Earl of Denver, *c.* 1450;
from a drawing at Bredon Hall

THE WIMSEY FAMILY

CONTENTS

ILLUSTRATIONS

THE WIMSEY FAMILY

I HOLD BY MY WHIMSY

THE SEARCH FOR WIMSEYS

S O LITTLE IS KNOWN of the family of Wimsey that had it not been for the writings of Miss Dorothy L. Sayers one might think that it never existed.

In 1923 Miss Sayers wrote the first of a series of books dealing with the activities of Lord Peter Wimsey, mainly in the field of criminal investigation, though we have glimpses of his scholarly interests such as the collection of

incunabula. The only members of the family mentioned
in the earlier books are Lord Peter; his brother, the Duke
of Denver, and the Duchess; his sister, Lady Mary; and
the Dowager Duchess. In the later books we meet the
Duke's son and heir, Viscount St. George, and a third
cousin, Mr Matthew Wimsey, the librarian and archivist
at Bredon Hall. In *Busman's Honeymoon* (1937) we read of
Lord Peter's marriage to Harriet Vane, and in a story
called 'Talboys', written in 1942 and published after Miss
Sayers's death, we find that Lord and Lady Peter have
three sons.

Only in *Busman's Honeymoon*, when Lord Peter shows
his wife round the picture gallery at Bredon Hall, do we
get hints at the long line of ancestors which a ducal
family might be expected to possess.

Probably Miss Sayers knew very little about the family
history when she began to write about the Wimseys of
her day. Lord Peter's brother, Gerald, was the 16th
Duke, whose predecessors, when they began to emerge,
went back to medieval times. And yet at his trial in the
House of Lords, in *Clouds of Witness* (1926), he is
described as 'a peer of the United Kingdom of Great
Britain and Ireland', which implies a creation after 2
July 1800. Only after Miss Sayers's death was attention
drawn to this apparent discrepancy, and it fell to me, as
the surviving student of the family history, to discover
the explanation; of which in its place.

While the Wimsey ancestry was still nebulous, Miss
Sayers provided the family with armorial bearings.
These were:

Arms: Sable, three mice courant argent.
Crest: A domestic cat couched as to spring, proper.
Supporters: Two Saracens armed proper.
Motto: I HOLD BY MY WHIMSY; sometimes AS MY WHIMSY
TAKES ME.

To a student of heraldry these bearings presented a
problem. They had the appearance of antiquity, and the
supporters seemed to indicate a crusading ancestor, but
the crest and arms were curiously pertinent to the
activities of the twentieth-century Lord Peter Wimsey in
keeping a cat-like watch at the mouse-holes of the
criminal world. I formed the personal opinion that the
arms and crest were ancient. However, wishing for an
authoritative view, on 16 February 1936 I put the matter
in a letter to Miss Sayers (whom I had not then met), and
suggested that for the information of the author of *Lord
Peter Wimsey—Man or Myth? (c.* 1990) some opportunity
should be found to explain that the arms were in fact
ancestral and that it was a matter of chance that they
reflected his criminological interests.

Two days later Miss Sayers replied:

The original arms of the Wimseys are held to have
been, Sable, three plates. Tradition asserts that the
Baron Fulk de Wimsey (or Guimsey) encouraged
King Richard I to persist in the siege of Acre, quoting
to him the analogy of the patience of a cat at a mouse-
hole; and that after the fall of the city the plates were
changed into silver mice in recognition of the baron's

good advice, the crest being assumed at the same time. It seems most likely, however, that the incident occurred during one of the later crusades, and was transferred to the earlier date by the antiquarian enthusiasm of the family chronicler. The plates and the mice occur interchangeably on tombstones and elsewhere during the thirteenth century. The tomb of Gerald, 5th Baron Wimsey (*d.* 1370) shows the effigy of a cat supporting the feet of the deceased, and by the time of the Wars of the Roses the animal is well established as the family crest, as is shown by the popular saying,

> When the Catt sits on the Bear's shoulder
> Craft doth make treason bolder,

in allusion to the notorious first Duke who was involved in the political intrigues of the King-maker.

The supporters appear first in a roll of arms of the time of Elizabeth; and the canting motto (which exists in two forms) is apparently due to the fanciful invention of seventeenth-century heralds.

(Later we found that the incident which resulted in the mice in the arms occurred during the Ninth Crusade, when Gerald de Wimsey accompanied Prince Edward, son of Henry III, on his expedition of 1270–2.)

Replying to this letter, I sent Miss Sayers a drawing of the Garter stall-plate (now missing from St. George's Chapel at Windsor) of 'le comte de Denver, Gerald de Guimsey'; and among other matters I advanced the theory that the rhyme, 'Three Blind Mice', who 'all ran after the Farmer's wife', was a lampoon dating from the reign of George III ('Farmer George') and referred to the Duke of Denver's unsuccessful pursuit of Queen Charlotte in soliciting a place in her household for one of his kinswomen. Miss Sayers replied that this fitted in with all she knew of the Wimsey family,

who at no time were above seeking political and territorial advantage from any royal condescension. They contrived to collar an extraordinary amount of confiscated Church property by taking the correct constitutional view of Henry VIII's divorce, and to hold on to it with singular tenacity during the troublesome reigns of Edward VI and Mary I, turning up (again on the right side) at the accession of Elizabeth

—who, however, was a match for the then Duke of Denver, as is told later.

So began a lively correspondence in which the Wimsey family history was gradually discovered. There was nothing systematic about it. We dodged about the centuries as ancestors and episodes occurred to us, but generally Miss Sayers found the Tudor and later Wimseys and I the medieval ones, especially those of heraldic interest. I made drawings of the fine monumental brass of Gerald, 1st Baron Wimsey (1300), the effigy on the tomb of the 5th Baron (1370), and his equestrian seal. Soon an ancestral pattern appeared, and on 25 March 1936 Miss Sayers wrote to me:

It is a curious fact that throughout the history of the family there have always been two Wimsey types, cropping up with extraordinary persistency. The commoner type is that of the present Duke and his father—bluff, courageous, physically powerful, honest enough, but rather stupid and entirely unimaginative, hearty eaters and swearers, *grands coureurs de filles*, and, if cruel, yet without malice or ingenuity. The other, occurring only sporadically and usually as the result of 'breeding out' into a foreign strain, is physically slighter, subtler, more intellectual and sensitive, with enormous nervous vitality, and with lusts no less powerful but more dangerously controlled to the furtherance of a long-sighted policy. To this type have belonged the wily statesmen and churchmen who have from time to time adorned the family tree; some of them have been notorious traitors, but here and there they have produced poets and saints.

The 1st Duke Peter, the friend of the King-maker, was of this type, and so was the Duke of Edward VI's time, who did so well for himself in the matter of Church property. But so, too, was the saintly Dr. Gervase Wimsey, Canon of St. Paul's, who embraced the new religion, and perished in the Marian persecutions; and that delicate and fastidious gentleman, scholar and poet, Lord Roger Wimsey, who was Sidney's friend and died, too young, of a 'wasting fever'; and the gentle eighteenth-century naturalist, Lord Paul, who lived in retirement in Dorset, writing innocent, and to this day valuable, notes on such subjects as the habits of the burying beetle and the melodic elements in the song of the missle-thrush (he was one of the musical ones); and that strange eccentric, Mortimer Wimsey, who in the rationalistic 1800s conceived himself to be one of the fish netted by St. Peter the Apostle, and lived many years alone in a hut on the sea-coast of Norfolk, wholly mute and eating nothing but shrimps and seaweed; until one morning, when the sun was rising over the North Sea, he beheld Christ walking on the waters and swam out to meet Him (as witness the narrative of the three peasant children who observed him), crying out in a melodious voice as he swam, 'Thou shalt open my lips, O Lord! The tongue of the dumb shall sing!'—whereby, many days afterwards, the Lowestoft trawlers brought up his body, along with a great draft of herrings ('so that their net brake'); and they buried him at the sea's edge, with the fishermen's net for his sole shroud; but the churchyard in no long time being undermined by the tides (as is common in those parts) the sea had him in the end, till St. Peter shall draw him home again at the Day of Judgement.

The women, too, fall into those two main types, the majority being energetic, amiable, faithful and fertile, and good practical housekeepers, busying themselves with their domestic affairs. But every so often they produce a portent, such as the infamous red-haired Marguerite la Saure, surnamed also le Succube, who was burned as a witch (*temp*. Henry VII) after seven husbands and innumerable lovers had perished of her insatiable appetite; or that dreadful old woman, Lady Stavesacre, who was an incurable litigious pest and boxed the ears of Bacon, the Lord Chancellor, when he gave judgement against her; or the Catholic nun, Mother Mary of the Immaculate Conception, who in 1632 sailed from France with a cargo of nuns and lepers to found a hospital colony on an island in the South Seas; or Mistress Lucasta Brand who, being condemned for high treason under Charles II, spoke such terrible and searching words to the Lord Chief Justice Jeffreys that even he was abashed at the sight of his own wicked heart thus stripped bare before him, and being choked with rage and terror fell down in a fit and had to be assisted from the court.

There have been, of course, intermediate types of all sorts, but these two recur continually. The physical characteristics, too, are very persistent. Peter's hands go back in the family portraits for three hundred years, and the fair colouring and beaked nose go back farther still, though in him they are exaggerated almost to the point of caricature. In fact if he had bred in, instead of (by good sense and fortune) breeding out into yeoman stock, one might be rather alarmed about the results for his descendants; in St. George, in spite of the steadying influence of the Delagardie blood, there is already a touch of instability, his father having married his own cousin.

Two months after my first letter to Miss Sayers we met for the first time. This was at lunch, and her friends Miss Helen Simpson and Miss Muriel St. Clare Byrne were also there. They too were drawn into the Wimsey research. We considered printing extracts from the growing historical material for the amusement of our friends, and at Christmas 1936 we produced a booklet entitled *Papers relating to the Family of Wimsey*. This dealt with the 'nine days' wonder' marriage, in 1751, of Viscount St. George, son of the 10th Duke of Denver. This was 'edited by Matthew Wimsey', who acknowledged the help given him by those who had prepared or contributed to the material, including Lord Peter Wimsey, Miss Sayers, Miss Simpson, Miss Byrne, myself and my wife. The booklet was privately printed 'for the family' by Humphrey Milford.

On 7 March 1937 Miss Sayers, Miss Simpson, Miss Byrne and I gave a group of papers on the Wimsey family to the Confraternitas Historica at Sidney Sussex College, Cambridge. I dealt with the medieval background and the heraldry. Miss Byrne gave the arguments for and against the theory that the Elizabethan Duke of Denver was associated with the Earl of Oxford in the authorship of some of the plays attributed to Shakespeare. Miss Simpson gave extracts from an eighteenth-century Household Book kept by Mary Wimsey, whose descendants were in New Zealand. Miss

Sayers gave the full story of Lord Mortimer Wimsey, outlined in her letter to me quoted above. At Christmas 1937 she sent her friends a pamphlet entitled *An Account of Lord Mortimer Wimsey, the Hermit of the Wash*, by 'A Clergyman of the Church of England'. This bore the date 1816. It has become a literary rarity. Extracts are given later.

Miss Sayers gave her own amusing account of our activities in a contribution to *Titles to Fame*, edited by D. K. Roberts (1937):

The course of English history is disturbed by the antics of dead-and-gone Wimseys, who leap from its waters like so many salmon in the mating season. My friends have become infected by my own madness; they wrestle valiantly with dates and genealogical trees and armorial bearings; they assist me to write spoof pamphlets about eighteenth-century Wimseys, adorned with plausible excerpts from Evelyn and Bubb Dodington and Horace Walpole; they embellish these fantasies with family portraits and contemporary views of Bredon Hall; they accept the existence of a poetical Wimsey who was a friend of Sir Philip Sidney, and meekly sit down to set his songs to music, while the local chemist prepares ink from an Elizabethan recipe wherewith I may forge the original manuscripts in a fair secretary hand. We discover Wimsey ciphers embedded in the plays of Shakespeare, and retrieve Wimsey commonplace books from remote corners of Australia; we sally forth in a team to foist these discoveries upon bewildered literary societies in respectable universities. I cannot imagine where all this is going to end.

So far as Miss Sayers was concerned it ended with a series of 'Wimsey Papers', being wartime letters and documents of the family, which appeared in the *Spectator* between November 1939 and January 1940. Then came the time when Miss Sayers, deep in more serious work, firmly said, 'There will be no more Peter Wimsey.'

Indeed, nothing more about the Wimseys appeared in her lifetime. She and I continued to meet fairly often, because she found I had a sufficient smattering of Dante, left over from my Cambridge days, to discuss debatable points in her translation of *The Divine Comedy*, and to draw the illustrations for it. However, I did not venture to mention the Wimseys, though their half-written history, in a thick file of letters, clamoured for completion.

In January 1959, a year after Miss Sayers's death, I contributed to the *Coat of Arms* (the journal of the Heraldry Society) an article on the Wimsey heraldry in which I told briefly how the history of the family had been compiled and gave extracts from the letters. Arising out of this, Mr. Valentine Heywood, author of *British Titles*, drew attention to the apparent discrepancy that the 16th Duke was described as 'a peer of the United Kingdom of Great Britain and Ireland', and so created after 2 July 1800, while the history showed that he came of a line of dukes, formerly earls, going back to the fifteenth century and properly described as 'peers of England'. I took the view that as Miss Sayers's Watson, and knowing her methods, I must regard her statements as correct, and if some of them appeared to be conflicting I must look for an hypothesis which would reconcile them. So I advanced the explanation that the 12th Duke died in 1817 leaving no heir to succeed to the dukedom, the earldom and the viscounty, which then became extinct. However, a few years later there was a second creation of a dukedom of Denver and a viscounty of St. George in a junior branch of the Wimsey family descended from a younger brother of the 1st Earl. The new peer was strictly the 1st Duke of the second creation, but as this was in the same family he was naturally regarded as and styled the 13th Duke. As Mr. Heywood raised no further question I assume he accepted the explanation. What Miss Sayers would have thought of the liberty I took with her Wimseys, I have no means of knowing.

There remains a quantity of unpublished material which I have now gathered together and put into chronological order. I have made a few additions of my own—for example, in connection with the creation of the second line of dukes. In some places I have enlarged on a mere hint by Miss Sayers, e.g. 'There was perhaps a Parliamentary Wimsey who contrived to keep things sweet under the Protectorate.' However, as a general rule I have left gaps in the record rather than create Wimseys unknown to Miss Sayers. The result is a fragmentary history, and one which deals at disproportionate length with certain characters who happen to be well documented, but it is thought that readers will welcome a summary of material which was privately printed and is difficult to find.

The surname Wimsey, though rare, is not unknown, and twice Miss Sayers was sent obituary notices of men called Peter Wimsey, one in Sligo and the other in Lancashire. 'It is curious', she wrote to me, 'that one can never invent a surname which does not exist.'

The view of Bredon Hall, based on a print c. 1740, was drawn by Mr. W. J. Redhead.

The portrait of the 10th Duke is not from the finished painting (attributed to Thomas Hudson) which hangs in the Gallery at Bredon Hall, but from a more revealing study in charcoal crayon which the artist made as a preliminary. This was restored and prepared for reproduction by my late wife.

The other illustrations are my own work.

C. W. S.-G.
Fitzalan

I

THE EARLY WIMSEYS

THE GREAT PEDIGREE of Wimsey ought to provide information about the origin and early history of the family, but unfortunately the upper membranes have been destroyed, evidently by fire, while the tattered state of the lower ones is clearly due to the ravages of rats. The mere fifteen feet which remain of this enormous document have at some time been stored in a damp place, and the manuscript is partly indecipherable. No copy of the missing parts exists, but from a note made by Sir William Dugdale we learn that the pedigree was drawn up in 1646, and traced the ancestry of the family to Adam, showing descent from Charlemagne and kinship with five others of the Nine Worthies, namely Hector, Alexander, Julius Caesar, King Arthur and Godfrey de Bouillon. Also, by an early marriage alliance with the Norfolk family of Heveningham, the Wimseys claimed descent from Arphaxad, described as one of the knights who watched Our Lord's sepulchre.

Disregarding apocryphal material, the first member of the family of whom we have record is Roger de Guimsey who followed Duke William in his invasion of England. Of his background in Normandy we know nothing, unless there be some truth in a legend associated with the original arms: Sable, three plates (i.e. silver roundels). This tells that the Sieur de Guimsey, a minor vassal of the Duke of the Normans, had three sons who, as they grew to manhood, became an intolerable burden by reason of their enormous appetites. That they usurped their father's *droit de seigneur* in respect of womenfolk mattered little, he having no further use for it; but when their Christmas feasting consumed the store of food and wine which should have lasted till Easter a serious situation arose. Accordingly, when Duke William summoned his vassals for the expedition against England, the Sieur de Guimsey welcomed the chance of ridding himself of his voracious sons. Calling them to him, he presented each with an empty platter which, he said, they should henceforth fill by their own efforts or go hungry. He added that English roast beef was said to be satisfying.

The brothers joined the Duke's army. What happened to the two younger is not known, though one of them, may have been the ancestor of the family de Wauncy, found in the rolls of arms bearing, sable, three gauntlets argent. The eldest brother, Roger, filled his plate with English fare, though being of small consequence among the many whom the Conqueror had to reward, he waited some years for a grant of English lands. He served in the expedition against Ely in 1071, when King William finally defeated Hereward, and Roger de Guimsey then received a manor in north-west Norfolk, on the edge of the fen country south of the Wash. His lands were bordered by the river Wissey, and this may

have been an influence in the gradual change of the
Norman name de Guimsey to the English form
'Wimsey'.

Roger's son, Fulk de Guimsey, made the first of a series
of prudent marriages by which, in a few generations, the
lands held by the family were greatly extended. Through
his wife he acquired a manor at Denver, near Downham
Market, which became the principal residence of the
Barons de Wimsey, and from which the title was taken
when they were created earls, and later dukes.
This Denver must not be confused with the village, about
fifteen miles to the north-east, containing Bredon Hall.
After the Wimseys acquired the Hall by marriage, and
eventually made it a ducal seat, the neighbouring village
came to be called Denver Ducis, or Duke's Denver.

Fulk de Guimsey had two sons: another Fulk who took
part in the Third Crusade, and Roger who was with
Henry II on his expedition to Ireland and became the
ancestor of the Irish Wimseys. Fulk II was the subject of a
legend recalled (or perhaps invented) by the Elizabethan
Kings-of-Arms when they granted two Saracens in
armour as supporters of the Denver shield. This told that
Fulk captured a noble and venerable Saracen chief and
held him for ransom. The chief's two sons offered
themselves in their father's place, and this was accepted.
Between Fulk and the two young men mutual respect
grew to friendship. One night Fulk was murderously
assailed by the servants of a personal enemy, and the
young Saracens came on the scene in the nick of time to
slay his attackers and save his life. There was no further

thought of ransom. The young men went free, and later Fulk received from the old chief a gold cup of Saracenic workmanship which became a family treasure.

Fulk II's son Peter de Guimsey was at the assembly at Bury St. Edmunds in 1214 when the draft of the Great Charter was drawn up, but took no conspicuous part and there is no record that he was at Runnymede. When, a year later, King John's army marched south from Lincoln, Peter found it wise to join the royal forces. As he well knew the Wash and its tides he was called on to guide the army across the sea marshes. It was, of course, no fault of his that there was an exceptionally high tide which swept away the King's baggage and treasure, but commmendably conscientious, and knowing where the flood waters usually deposited flotsam, he and his men undertook to look for the missing property. Presumably they were unsuccessful, since there is no record that the valuables were ever returned to the royal treasury. Nevertheless, in the 1850s a discovery was made which may have a bearing on the matter. A Norfolk antiquary, poking about the ruins of the castle near Bredon Hall, found projecting from the soil the corner of an oaken chest. Unearthed and opened, this was found to contain three articles—a cup, a plate, and a gold circlet mounted with four fleurs-de-lis. The finder is said to have handed these over to the then Duke of Denver, the owner of the land where they were found. As no inquest was held, the Duke presumably took the view that the articles were ancestral property. In 1936 Mr. Matthew Wimsey, the person most likely to know, could throw no light on what had become of them, but thought they might be in some forgotten recess at Bredon Hall. Lord Peter, asked to exercise his detective powers, could only say that finding the articles might entail pulling the Hall to pieces (which might not be a bad thing); but if ever they should turn up they should be expertly examined and, if found to date from the thirteenth century, offered to the Crown for display with the regalia at the Tower of London.

Peter's son, Roger de Wimsey (as the name now became), was a supporter of Simon de Montfort, and as such was at variance with his own eldest son, Gerald, who was an adherent to Prince Edward. Gerald fought for the Prince at Evesham, and this is thought to have saved his father the heavy fine which Henry III imposed on Simon's followers. This was the first instance of what became family policy—that in times of civil strife there should be a Wimsey in each camp so that the one on the winning side might help to extricate his kinsman from the consequences of backing the loser.

Gerald became the 1st Baron de Wimsey, and is dealt with below. His younger brother, Ralph, was a scholar at Oxford where, coming under the influence of Roger Bacon, he developed a questioning mind, and dabbled in astronomy and alchemy. Had he been content with a theoretical study of these unorthodox matters, the authorities might merely have frowned their disapproval, but when he boldly asserted that the calendar was in error having regard to astronomical reckoning, and ought to be reformed, he incurred the wrath of the Church and was imprisoned for heresy.

II

THE BARONS DE WIMSEY

AFTER EVESHAM, Gerald de Wimsey was with Prince
Edward in the campaign against the remnant of de
Montfort's supporters, and helped to round up those who
had taken refuge in the fens near Ely. He then took part
in the Prince's crusade (1270–2) and was present when
Nazareth was taken from the infidels. It must have been
on some occasion during this crusade that de Wimsey
counselled Prince Edward to imitate the patience of a cat
watching a mouse-hole, for about this time—
presumably with the Prince's approval—he changed the
plates in his shield to mice and took the domestic cat as
his crest.

Gerald was rewarded for his faithful service when
Edward became king. In 1289 he received the personal
writ of summons to Parliament, and so became the 1st
Baron de Wimsey. Nine years later he was with the King
in the Scottish expedition to put down William
Wallace's rising, and took part in the battle of Falkirk.
This was his last campaign, for he died in 1300 a little
before the attack on Caerlaverock castle, so that his shield
is not found in the rhyming roll of arms compiled on that
occasion.

Monumental brass of Gerald de Wimsey, 1st Baron, *d.* 1300;
at Duke's Denver

The first Baron's magnificent monumental brass shows him lying fully armed, with his legs crossed and a domestic cat at his feet. The courant mice appear on his shield, surcoat and ailettes, while the old arms—the three plates—occur on four small shields forming the decoration of the scabbard.

Gerald's son Roger, the 2nd Baron, somehow avoided the dangerous situations of Edward II's reign. He was not at Bannockburn, not with the army that opposed Bruce's invasion of northern England, and not among the barons who deposed the King. His two sons, Peter (who died childless) and Ralph, the 3rd and 4th Barons, were among those Wimseys, found in every generation, who made the care and increase of their patrimony their first concern. Their principal residence was still at Denver, but their lands now extended many miles to the north-eastward, where they marched with those of the family of Bredon.

The estates and standing of the Wimsey family were greatly increased as a result of the marriage of Ralph's son, Gerald, to Margaret, daughter and heiress of Sir Thomas Bredon. Thereafter the Wimseys made Bredon Hall their chief residence, and the near-by church the place where their funeral monuments joined those of the Bredons. Gerald built a small but strong castle in the vicinity. This was known as Denver Castle when the neighbouring village came to be called Duke's Denver.

Gerald, who became 5th Baron Wimsey, was born in 1307. He served in France under Edward, 'the Black

Seal of Gerald de Wimsey, 5th Baron, *c.* 1350

Prince', and Miss Sayers found a reference to him in Froissart's account of the siege of Rennes (1357), though this occurs only in a fragmentary copy of the chronicle in the possession of the Earl of Severn and Thames. The Froissart extract communicated to me by Miss Sayers was in Old French. The following is my translation:

> . . . And there too was my Lord Giraut de Guimsey, who was reputed to be the proudest of all the barons of England, and was very doughty and valiant in arms though he was already fifty years old. And he bore a shield of sable with three white mice, and on his helm a couchant cat of the kind called 'cat du fouier' [i.e. hearth-side or domestic cat] which was his device. Now, there came a day during the siege when Messire de Guimsey came riding before the gate of the city, armed at all points and bearing himself very haughtily.

Above the gate there was a young captain of the Constable's company, who was a very presumptuous man. And it so happened that this captain picked out the Baron as he rode by, and from the height of the wall threw down at him the stinking body of a dead cat, saying, 'Hi, old cat! Go and mouse by the hearth, for this is no place for you!' Then said Messire du Guesclin, who heard him, 'when the cat's away the mice will play! [La ou caz n'est li souris se revele] Upon my word, it is unbecoming a knight to insult a lord of such high lineage and so renowned for prowess!' Then cried Messire de Guimsey, 'To your holes, you mice! For if you dare to come out and fight with me, you will find that the old cat has claws to tear you with!' 'Alas!' said the Constable. 'For a mean remark we shall all be shamed.' Then Messire du Guesclin offered to fight against my Lord de Guimsey, who was delighted at this. Then the Constable came down from the walls and, getting into a small boat, crossed the moat. And Messire de Guimsey alighted from his horse and set himself on foot. And for a long time the Baron de Guimsey and the Constable of France fought hand to hand, and gave such a great display of their skill in arms that all marvelled at it. Then Messire de Guimsey was sorely wounded in the right arm, and Messire du Guesclin in the shoulder. And at nightfall, when neither had the advantage of the other, they saluted one another most courteously. Then said the Constable, 'Now I see well that no man can contrive to correct an old cat, for the cats of

Effigy on the tomb of Gerald de Wimsey, 5th Baron,
d. 1370; at Duke's Denver

England are lions for valour!' And Messire de Guimsey replied, 'A bon cat, bon rat!' Then each withdrew to his own following. And this was held to be a notable passage of arms.

On his seal Gerald de Wimsey is shown fully armed and on horseback, with the courant mice on his shield, surcoat and the bardings of his horse, and the cat couchant on his helm. On the effigy on his tomb the mice appear on the shield and surcoat, and also in the decoration of the sword belt. His head rests on his great helm mounted with the crest of the couchant cat, while there is a recumbent cat at his feet.

He left three sons—Ralph who succeeded him, Roger and Peter. Roger became a fellow of Balliol College, Oxford, during the mastership of John Wycliffe and later was one of his 'poor preachers'. Peter was the ancestor of a line of Wimseys—knights and squires in East Anglia—who remained in close touch with their kinsmen at Bredon Hall. One of these was Colonel John Wimsey, the Parliamentarian, from whom descended the 1st Duke of Denver of the second creation.

III

THE EARLS OF DENVER

RALPH, 6TH BARON WIMSEY, was a member of the Parliament which, in 1399, accepted the abdication of Richard II and declared Henry IV to be his successor. Soon afterwards he was created Earl of Denver, but he did not enjoy the honour for long, dying in 1405. For him was made the Denver missal, preserved at Bredon Hall. I am indebted to Miss Sayers for this description:

On the first page the Earl is depicted dressed in an extremely rich houppelande lined with miniver, an enormous chaperon and shoes of great length, presenting his Countess (also very fashionably attired) and his three sons to our Blessed Lady in the stable at Bethlehem, under the admiring gaze of St. Joseph, St. Thomas of Canterbury and two Archangels. In the margin the Wimsey white mice and the tabby cat pursue one another through the intricacies of some conventional foliage. The presence of St. Thomas in the composition suggests that it may commemorate a pilgrimage to his shrine at Canterbury.

The 1st Earl's three sons, Gerald, Ralph and Roger,

succeeded in turn to the earldom, the two elder dying childless.

Gerald, 2nd Earl of Denver, may be said to have enjoyed the title 'Earl of Hell', for he found a grim pleasure in the form and significance given to his name by the French. He went to France with Henry V in 1415, and was one of those left to garrison Harfleur when the main army went forward. After Agincourt he was fiercely active in putting an end to any resistance by castles and towns in northern France, and such was his savagery that men called him 'le comte d'Enfer', and sometimes 'le chat d'Enfer'. A French chronicler wrote that he moused like a hunting cat:

le comte d'Enfer
Sourisoit comme un chat chasseur,

words which have come down through the centuries, though by the omission of one letter from 'sourisoit' and by the distortion of 'chasseur' they have become the otherwise inexplicable phrase, 'grinned like a Cheshire cat'.

How the Earl's career of rapine came to an end is a matter of legend which may contain some element of truth. Coming one day to a castle which he expected to find undefended, knowing its lord to be dead, he found the ports shut and the walls manned, and a vehement young priest over the gateway loudly urging the garrison to hold the castle for God against the Devil and his emissary the Earl of Hell. When Denver approached and offered his usual terms, 'Surrender or hang', the priest, having his spiritual weapon at hand, tipped a bucket of holy water over him, crying, 'Chat d'Enfer, get thee back to thy master!' What followed was short and bloody. The castle fell and the priest was brought before Denver. 'Hang him,' said the Earl, and when someone murmured that the prisoner was a man of God, 'Then he'll go straight to Heaven,' he added. As he was led away, the priest shouted words which the Earl heeded little though others recalled them later: 'Foul son of Satan, the days of your oppression are numbered. The mice you have preyed on shall turn and plague you to your undoing, and in that hour your hell-cat shall not avail you!'

A few days later Denver, in armour, was riding to attack a small town, when he began to feel an irritation in several parts of his body, and particularly in his scalp. This became unbearable, and he was forced to dismount and, with the help of his squires, remove his armour. When they took off his bascinet two large mice leaped out of it and disappeared, and as they stripped off his mail shirt six or seven more of the creatures darted out. This began a murrain of mice which put an end to the Earl's career as a warrior. He could shake the pests out of his clothes and his bed, but when he donned his armour—each piece carefully searched and found free of mice—there they materialized and drove him frantic in their attempts to escape from confinement.

Inevitably the Earl's visitation became known, and soon men associated it with the hanged priest's curse. The mice had indeed turned on him, and his cat did not avail

him, for these were mice which no cat would notice or
pounce on. Some whispered that no man saw the mice
but Denver himself. Real or imagined, they made it
impossible for him to wear armour, and soon he was no
longer the dreaded 'comte d'Enfer' but a figure of fun
nicknamed 'le chat vermineux'. He left France and went
into retirement at Bredon Hall. Here his confessor, who
had heard something of the story, persuaded him to do
penance and to have masses said for the priest and his
other victims, but he never again wore mail, and could
not bear the sight of the Wimsey mice on his shield and
surcoat. He died a few months after his return home, and
his brother Ralph succeeded to the earldom.

It has been plausibly suggested that some faint memory
of Denver's murrain of mice was in the mind of the
White Knight when he carried a mouse-trap on his
horse's back. It was not likely there would be mice there,
'but if they *do* come I don't choose to have them running
all about.'

When I found the foregoing legend and sent it to Miss
Sayers, she expressed the opinion that the story of the
murrain of mice had some significance not at once
apparent. She asked Lord Peter to consult Mr. Matthew
Wimsey about it next time he was at Bredon Hall, and a
few days later she sent me the result of this inquiry:

According to Cousin Matthew, the unsavoury epithets
applied to the 'comte d'Enfer' are a matter of historical
fact, and he, with some modest hesitation, has put
forward a theory of his own, viz. that the priest's curse

('The mice you have preyed on shall turn and plague you') may have been symbolically fulfilled, though possibly not in the sense that the priest foresaw. Not to put too fine a point on it, the Earl, having in his career of rapine *chassé dans des trous sales*, returned home suffering from various unpleasant maladies, and (here, says Peter, Cousin Matthew paused and took snuff in a deprecating manner) died shortly after of the pox. At this Peter burst out laughing, clapped Cousin Matthew on the shoulder, and exhorted him to cheer up, since after all it was a very long while ago, and the disease had had time to wear itself out.

By one of those contrasts frequent in the Wimsey family, Ralph, the 3rd Earl, was a saintly and celibate scholar. While the 2nd Earl was absent in France and the 3rd aloof from worldly affairs, their younger brother Roger husbanded the now extensive property, and well defended it in that litigious period, and so continued when he succeeded to the earldom. Roger's son, Gerald, the 5th Earl, was less fortunate. Unwillingly but inevitably he was drawn into the dynastic struggle between York and Lancaster, and he and his son Peter—already a friend of the young Earl of Warwick—fought at Wakefield, where Denver was slain.

Peter, now the 6th Earl, escaped after the battle, firmly resolved that the fate which had overtaken his father should never be his. Henceforth his guiding principle was that, whether York or Lancaster should prevail,

Denver should survive, if possible with advancement. Of his association with Warwick it was said:

> When the Catt sits on the Bear's shoulder
> Craft doth make treason bolder.

This must have been put about by Warwick's enemies since it describes his activities as treason. But while whispering in Warwick's ear, Denver was receptive to whispers in his own, and he knew when the moment had come to jump off the Bear's shoulder. He joined Edward IV in the campaign which ended in Warwick's defeat and death. Later he acquiesced in Richard of Gloucester's seizure of the throne; but perhaps he heard and heeded the warning Jockey of Norfolk ignored—'Diccon thy master is bought and sold'—for on the eve of Bosworth he joined Henry of Richmond.

That night, from King Richard's camp, the ardent Yorkist Lord Humber sent Denver a hangman's rope, with the message that he would do well to accustom himself to its feel. Denver sent back the rope knotted into a noose, with a paper bearing the words, *Nodus tibi non mihi*. Humber's death in next day's battle prevented Denver carrying out the implied threat, but as a warning to his enemies he adopted the noose as one of his badges, and, known as the Wimsey knot, it is still among the family devices (though not one favoured by the 16th Duke).

Early in Henry VII's reign Earl Peter was created Duke of Denver, perhaps helped thereto by a handsome gift to the royal treasury.

Meanwhile Denver's younger brother Ralph had followed the useful, unspectacular course of looking after the estates. He was the first of the Wimseys to take an interest in the control of the fenland waters, and joined Bishop Morton of Ely in an attempt at fen drainage. This was not very successful, but it represents an early concern with a problem which later engaged the attention of Lord Peter Wimsey, as told in *The Nine Tailors* (1934).

IV

THE DUKES OF DENVER

DUKE PETER, having realized his ambition to survive the dynastic war, and gained advancement thereby, loyally supported Henry Tudor (though privately thinking little of his ancestral background), and had the good fortune, rare in a nobleman of his time, to spend the last years of his life in the peaceful enjoyment of his estates. He died in 1499 and was buried in a magnificent tomb in the church at Duke's Denver.

It is remarkable that the Denvers survived the perils of ducal rank in the sixteenth century. Buckingham, Somerset and Suffolk were in turn attainted and beheaded, and when in 1572 Norfolk met the same fate, leaving a son with no higher title than Earl of Arundel, Denver became England's only duke, and so remained for the rest of Elizabeth's reign. The survival of the Wimsey dukedom was initially due to the fact that the family had no royal blood, and so was not a menace to the Tudor dynasty. Furthermore the Denvers were individually cautious, and in times of political perplexity were wont to fall 'crafty sick' or find some other reason for retiring to one of their country seats. Richard, the 2nd Duke, kept no band of liveried retainers such as Henry

VII frowned on. Roger, the 3rd, found no difficulty of conscience in accepting the tortuous policies of Henry VIII which led to the reformation of the Church, and the dispersal of the monastic lands, of which a large share came Denver's way. When Edward VI died, Duke Roger's brother, Lord Henry, 'raised the standard for Queen Mary in Norfolk at her accession' (*vide* Lord Peter Wimsey in *Busman's Honeymoon*), but this did not save the third brother, Dr. Gervase Wimsey, Canon of St. Paul's, from martyrdom for his Protestant convictions.

At the accession of Queen Elizabeth, Gerald, the 4th Duke of Denver, was prompt to wait on her at Hatfield, full of loyal acknowledgements of favours to come. He was much at court, usually attended by a group of members of the Wimsey family or one of its satellites. On their behalf the Duke was constantly solicitous for places, patents, monopolies and other means of revenue. At last, however, he exhausted the Queen's patience, and received a royal rebuke. This was found by Miss Sayers in a hitherto unedited volume of Harington's memoirs:

My lord of Denver, at many times requiring of her (the Queen) divers places about her household for the gentlemen of his kin, and in especial for his sister, my lady Grenehowe, to be made mistress of the Spicery, her Grace flew into a great passion, saying, 'Our household? Our household? God's death, my lord Duke, we must look to our housekeeping, for with the mice in the barn and the cat in the pantry, we are likely to be eaten out of house and home!' Whereat my lord, knowing the Queen's stomach, and having no mind to provoke her to further choler, withdrew himself from the court on the excuse of a sudden distemper.

The Duke found it politic to present the Queen, on her next birthday, with a manor in Warwickshire and a handsome new dress of cloth of gold embroidered with great pearls.

There was one man who held that that Warwickshire manor was not Denver's to give. This was John Shakespeare, of Stratford-upon-Avon. His grandfather, for faithful and valiant service to Henry VII, had been advanced and rewarded with lands and tenements in Warwickshire—or so the records said, but John's father told him, and John told his son, that the second Duke of Denver had trumped up some claim to the manor intended for the Shakespeares, and they had never received it. Probably John did not seriously consider taking legal proceedings against a powerful nobleman, but he liked to think and tell his friends about a landed estate which was his by rights. The 4th Duke may well have known that his title to this manor was questionable, and therefore chose it when he found it advisable to make a gift of land to the Queen.

John and his son, William, were angered that their rightful property should thus be handed over to a recipient from whom it could never be recovered, and the Duke of Denver was henceforth regarded as the Shakespeares' nearest and dearest enemy. So when

William wrote *Romeo and Juliet* he attacked Denver in the character of Tybalt, 'more than Prince of Cats'.

> *Mercutio*. Tybalt, you rat-catcher, will you walk?
> *Tybalt*. What wouldst thou have with me?
> *Mercutio*. Good King of Cats, nothing but one of your nine lives; that I mean to make bold withal, and, as you shall use me hereafter, dry-beat the rest of the eight.

They fight, and Mercutio, mortally wounded, exclaims, 'Zounds! a dog, a rat, a mouse, a cat, to scratch a man to death!' A few minutes later Tybalt falls in a fight with Romeo, and Shakespeare has the satisfaction of knowing he will dry-beat Denver every time the play is acted.

Lord Peter, showing his wife round Bredon Hall (in *Busman's Honeymoon*) told her, 'Queen Elizabeth slept here in the usual way, and nearly bust the family bank.' This was probably in the time of the 4th Duke. He was succeeded by Henry, the 5th Duke, whom Lord Peter described as 'one of the tedious Wimseys, and greed was his leading characteristic', but this reputation may be due to necessary measures to restore the family finances after the Queen's expensive visit.

The 4th Duke's younger children included Lord Roger, Sir Philip Sidney's friend, and Lady Stavesacre, both mentioned in Miss Sayers's letter of 25 March 1936, and also referred to in *Busman's Honeymoon*.

Of Lord Roger's poetry little has come down to us. However, Miss Sayers discovered the manuscript of a few songs, and a series of verses entitled 'The Zodiac', consisting of twelve sonnets each devoted to a month of the year. I have transcribed the following song from a manuscript which has the appearance of being in a sixteenth-century hand, and written in ink of that period.

SONGE FOR VOYCE AND LUTE

As drizling water wears the stone
So hope my harte doth waste.
Fy on thee, fy.
It was not kindlie done
To lett mee languisshe soe.
These torments are too slowe.
Haste then, haste,
And O for pittie, for pittie, for pittie,
Burne mee up and lett mee dye,
For fyre destroyeth faste.

Griefe hath noe sicknesse, hath noe paine,
That can with hope compaire.
Too cruel kinde,
Give mee my griefe agayne,
Nor dwindle out my woes
With these fair seeming showes.
Fair, be faire,
And O for pittie, for pittie, for pittie,
Kill my hope, my harte, my minde,
And leave mee to dispaire.

ROGER WIMSEY
1583

Another son of the 4th Duke was Lord Christian, who sailed with Francis Drake, though the reports of his career are scanty and conflicting. He was first mentioned in a letter from Miss Sayers in May 1936. She gave him no first name but said he was 'not the Lord Roger who was Sidney's friend but a robuster kind of young man altogether. I think he survived the Armada, and was killed in Essex's disastrous expedition before Corunna.'

The only other reference to a Wimsey shipmate of Drake occurs in a letter from the Dowager Duchess of Denver to Lady Peter Wimsey, communicated by Miss Sayers to the *Spectator*, 22 December 1939. Loved and respected though she was, Lord Peter's mother cannot be taken as a very accurate witness in a matter of family history, and in a letter she would no doubt have relied on memory without checking her statements. This should be remembered in connection with the following extract:

. . . When I think of some of the Elizabethan Wimseys—the third Lord Christian, for example, who could write four languages at eleven, left Oxford at fifteen, married at sixteen, and had two wives and twelve children by the time he was thirty (two lots of twins, certainly, but it's all experience) besides producing a book of elegies and a learned exhibition [Qy disquisition? D.L.S.] on Leviathans, and he would have done a great deal more, I dare say, if he hadn't unfortunately been killed by savages on Drake's first voyage to the Indies—I sometimes feel that our young people don't get enough out of life these days.

The 2nd, 3rd and 4th Dukes all had a Lord Christian among their younger sons. I think that in this letter the Dowager Duchess confused two of these. Probably it was the second Lord Christian who was twice married, prolific, an elegist and an authority on leviathans, and his nephew, the third Christian, was the robust young man who sailed with Drake. There remains the question whether this Lord Christian perished on Drake's voyage to the West Indies in 1570, or whether he survived to take part in the action against the Armada and in Essex's expedition of 1597. I find the latter version more acceptable as coming direct from Miss Sayers.

On the monument of the 4th Duke the two Saracens first appear as the supporters of the Wimsey arms. The armorial bearings have received no attention from heraldic writers, though one might expect to find them in such a book as John Guillim's *Display of Heraldrie*. So some member of the family seems to have thought, for a copy of Guillim (second edition, 1632) in the library at Bredon Hall contains an added page bearing the following note in manuscript:

He beareth, Sable, three Mice courant Argent, by the name of Wimsey. This is the Paternall Coat of the Right Noble the Duke of Denver. The bearing of the Mouse doth signifie nimblenesse of wit, for though nature hath not given these timorous kinds of beasts strength or weapons to wound their foes, yet have they great agilitie; and as it is told of the Mouse that with its sharpe teeth it did liberate the Lion from the net, so

may he who beareth this charge bring succour and
counsell to the Soveraygne in his adversitie.
Furthermore the Mouse is proper to him that is expert
in enriching himself at the cost of others, for this
creature hath such craft that it can take the bait yet
avoid the trap. And note that this family of Wimsey do
beare for crest a domestick Cat couching as to spring,
in token that to the swiftnesse and cunning of the
Mouse they join the vigilance and ferocitie of the
Mouser.

There seems to be no inn bearing the name and sign of
The Wimsey Arms, but the crest and Saracen supporters
may have given rise to the inn name, The Cat and Infidel,
usually found in the corrupt form, The Cat and Fiddle.

Of Christian, the 6th Duke of Denver, little is known.
At the outbreak of the Civil War he was too advanced in
years to take an active part, but his son, Paul, was prompt
to join the King, and served in the royal army while it
remained an effective force. He then joined Prince
Charles in Scotland, marched with him into England,
and fought at Worcester. After that final defeat of the
royalist cause, he rode with a group of comrades to the
Dorset coast. There they managed to borrow a lugger
which Lord Paul, accustomed to sailing off the north
coast of Norfolk, was well able to handle, and the party
escaped to France.

Bredon Hall, deep in the eastern counties dominated
by the Parliamentary forces, could not be a centre of
royalist activity. Nevertheless, the Earl of Manchester,

knowing the Duke and his household were firmly for the King, decided that someone should be appointed to keep a watchful eye on the place. Perhaps to show that even among the Wimseys there were good Parliamentarians, he chose for the task Colonel John Wimsey, who had been wounded at Naseby and was now available for non-combatant duties. The Colonel was very distantly connected with the Duke of Denver, being a descendant of the 1st Earl's younger brother. He came to Duke's Denver with a small troop of horse, and orders to garrison the place and see that nobody entered Bredon Hall without giving an account of himself.

Colonel Wimsey had one private interview with the Duke, after which they met only in the presence of other people, and were distantly courteous to one another. Life in the household and on the estates went quietly on, remote from scenes of warfare. The Colonel showed himself zealous in the Parliamentary cause. At his suggestion what was left of the old castle at Duke's Denver was demolished. This was no great loss to the Wimseys. The castle had last been put in a state of defence during Ket's rebellion in 1549, and since then it had been used as a storehouse, but its destruction showed Colonel Wimsey's superiors that he was alert and active.

The Colonel was conscientious in seeing that any stranger who came to the gates of Bredon Hall was stopped and questioned. What he could not do, with his handful of men, was to ensure that no one came to the place by night, through the farm tracks and field paths leading to the Peddar's Way that ran northwards to the sea-coast. Sometimes, unknown to him, a vessel dropped anchor off Brancaster or Holkham, and a messenger came across country to Bredon Hall with news of the Duke's son at the Prince's court in exile. Occasionally a Captain Brown, master of a ship trading with the Low Countries, threaded the secluded paths from the coast and appeared at Bredon Hall at nightfall, to be admitted by some side door or window and to leave the house in the early morning. Since he was last in those parts he had grown a full beard, and in seaman's clothes was not likely to be recognized, but he was very cautious, not so much for his own safety as to avoid bringing danger to those he visited.

Early in 1653, a few days after one of Captain Brown's fleeting appearances, Duke Christian died, and in due course the news reached Paul that he was now the 7th Duke. Colonel Wimsey continued to represent the authority of the State at Duke's Denver, mixing mainly with others of his political persuasion, and remaining formal in his relations with the widowed Duchess and her family at Bredon Hall. However, there was no doubt that this quiet, correct man, watchdog though he was, made life easier for the Wimseys than it was for some of their royalist neighbours. He saw that the State's decrees were observed and its taxes paid, but he also interested himself in the good management of the property, and as time passed he became increasingly aware of his own kinship with the family, distant though it was. He was also one of many Parliamentarians who were dis-illusioned by the oppressive government of recent years.

Then came the news that the Lord Protector was dead, and a confused period of doubt as to the future of the Commonwealth and of those who served it. Early in the new regime Colonel Wimsey's small troop was posted for duty elsewhere, and he himself was told to remain at Duke's Denver and await further orders. One day he was informed that a Captain Brown wished to see him. When the visitor appeared the Colonel at once knew him, though it was many years since they had met. What passed between them can only be guessed, but no doubt Captain Brown thanked the Colonel for the way in which, while carrying out his military duties, he had seen that no harm came to the family and the estates, while the Colonel may have admitted to a growing regard for his distant kinsfolk. Perhaps Captain Brown gave an inkling of what brought him to England, and revealed that he was on his way to see the Colonel's old chief, the Earl of Manchester, long since estranged from Cromwell and living in retirement at Kimbolton.

Now that he was no longer in command at Duke's Denver, Colonel Wimsey felt able to meet the family on social terms, and he took particular pleasure in the company of the Duke's youngest sister, Lady Elizabeth. Later that year the prospect of the restoration of the monarchy began to be discussed, though not until May 1660 did Prince Charles return to England to mount the throne. With him came Paul, Duke of Denver, to take his place in the House of Lords when its Speaker, the Earl of Manchester, delivered a loyal address to the Sovereign.

A few days later the Duke returned to Bredon Hall amid the rejoicing of his family and tenants. When he enquired for Colonel Wimsey he was told he was now living with his parents about twelve miles away, and he sent a message that Captain Brown would like the Colonel to join the festivities at Bredon Hall. Later that year Colonel Wimsey and Lady Elizabeth were married. Their descendants are dealt with later in this record.

For his services to Charles II, Duke Paul was made a Knight of the Garter, and Hereditary Keeper of the Privy Stair. The actual duties of this office were carried out by Chiffinch and his successors, but the Denvers valued the titular appointment and claimed it in later reigns. However, at her accession Queen Victoria expressed the view that if there must be such an office it should now be held by a woman, and to avoid embarrassing Her Majesty with explanations the Duke gallantly dropped his claim. It has not been renewed in this century.

Duke Paul married Frances Montagu, of a family connected with the Earl of Manchester, and they had a daughter, but the Duke was advised that there would be no more children. His heir presumptive was Lord Peter, his half-brother by their father's second marriage, to the daughter of the last Lord St. George. In order that his heir might have a title suited to his station and prospects, Duke Paul persuaded Charles II to create Peter Viscount St. George, and when in due course Peter succeeded as Duke, St. George became the courtesy title used by his eldest son, and so continued in later generations.

Court life did not appeal to Duke Paul, and after his years of warfare, exile and adventure he was thankful for peaceful country pursuits. He made improvements at Bredon Hall (the stones of the castle which Colonel Wimsey had knocked down coming in very useful as building material), and during the Duke's leisure 'Captain Brown' reappeared off the Norfolk coast as the owner of a yacht. His frequent companion on sea-going expeditions was his nephew Henry, who was thus attracted to a career in the Navy, served under Admiral Russell in the defeat of the French fleet off La Hogue, and was the father and grandfather of naval officers. In the 1760s Captain Wimsey, living in retirement at Burnham Overy, was noted locally for a wealth of adventurous sea stories, and it is said that among the young people who listened to his yarns was Horatio, son of Mr. Nelson, rector of neighbouring Burnham Thorpe.

Paul died in 1677 and Peter became the 8th Duke. He continued the work of improving and extending Bredon Hall. There is an undated account of a visit to the place among the miscellaneous papers left by John Evelyn, but not entered in his diary. As Evelyn is known to have been in Norfolk in October 1671 it was thought that he visited Bredon Hall at that time, but it has now been found that the Lord Richard who received him was born in 1663, so that his visit is likely to have been about 1685. The account is as follows:

We went to see the mansion-house and gardens of the

Duke of Denver. My Lord being from home, we were received by his son, Lord Richard Wimsey, a very discreet and ingenious gentleman who, having no inclination to the buffoonery and prophanenesse of Court, chooses rather to busy himself in contriving to improve and adorn the seat. Would that as much could be said of his elder brother, the lord St. George, who is much given to gaming and other horrid vices. The house has a sweet prospect, being very well situated on rising grounds, environ'd with fertile, woody and well-water'd country, and having a goodly avenue of oaks up to it. There are noble terraces and walks, with some modern statues, but more nakeds than I thought seemly. His Lordship advis'd with me as to his project for a grotto and waterworks, and spoke of adding an orangery, conservatory and decoy.

The house is a mixed fabric, the greater part of the age of Henry VIII and Queen Elizabeth, to which, having fallen into disrepair in the late unnatural war, the Duke has added a facciata and porticos in imitation of a house in Palladio's book. The tympanum over the entrance is a bass-relievo of Jupiter and Leda. The dining room is richly painted à fresco by Signor Verrio, and the rest of the lodgings answerable, with a noble gallery wainscoted in Spanish oak and a pretty chapel. They have some good pictures of their ancestors by the best masters, especially some Vandykes and an incomparable head of the 3rd Duke by H. Holbein. In the library there is a good collection of books, many richly bound and gilded, and some valuable manu-

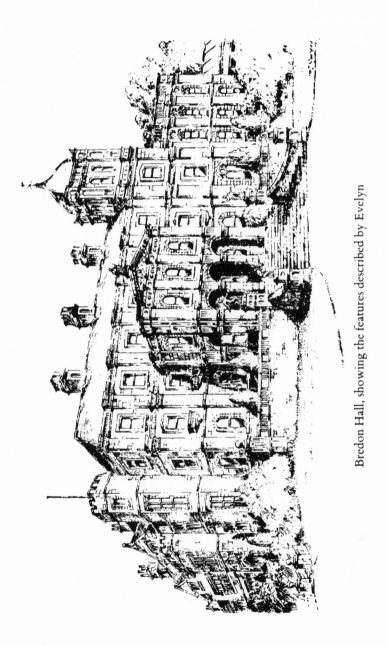

Bredon Hall, showing the features described by Evelyn

scripts. I observ'd there my French Gardener and Sylva.

Neere to the house is a church wherein are chantries with tombs of the Wimsey and Bredon families. These parts of the fabric are in very good repair. But the rest sadly ruinous, that it seems there is greater care of the repositories for the dead than of the house of God, but Lord Richard assur'd me that work on rebuilding the church will soon begin.

Some of the features observed by Evelyn are shown in the drawing of Bredon Hall included in *Papers relating to the Family of Wimsey* (1936).

Duke Peter married Joan Steward, of a family which started as Styward, changed to Steward and, in Henry VIII's reign, claimed descent from the High Stewards of Scotland and thereby a connection with the Royal House of Stewart. This piece of genealogical fantasy seems to have been initiated by Robert Steward, last Prior and first Dean of Ely. Within a few years a detailed pedigree supporting it was concocted, and in 1575 this was put on record by Robert Cooke, Clarenceux King-of-Arms. This pedigree has been demolished by modern scholars (*vide* J. H. Round, *The Origin of the Stewarts*, 1900) but it was accepted as fact in the seventeenth and eighteenth centuries, and led the Wimseys to believe that they had a common ancestor with the Stewart kings. Nevertheless, Duke Peter was glad to see the back of James II, and joined in the welcome to William of Orange and Mary; and in due course his son accepted George I as King, though with little enthusiasm. However, Duke Peter's youngest son, Walter, displayed some regard for 'King James III' in exile, and brought up his son James to drink to the King across the water.

Had the Jacobite forces come south of Lancashire in 1715, Walter might have joined them. James Wimsey is said to have been one of a group of men who planned to demonstrate their Stewart sympathies at the coronation of George II by picking up the gauntlet flung down by the King's Champion in the traditional ceremony at Westminster Hall. But the authorities seem to have got wind of their intentions, for when the day came the Champion was so surrounded by a press of heralds, pursuivants, yeomen of the guard and other functionaries that no one could push his way through to take up the challenge. In 1745 James set out with the intention of joining Prince Charles Edward but did not reach him before he turned back at Derby. Sympathy for the Stewart cause lingered on among some members of the family, and Miss Sayers told me that Mr. Matthew Wimsey 'in a mumbling and harmless way, proclaims himself a Jacobite, and puts white roses on the statue of Charles I'.

George, the 9th Duke, married Charlotte Death, of a family related to the baronets who spelt their name 'D'Aeth'. (There was another and later Wimsey–Death marriage which led to Death being given to Lord Peter Wimsey as his second Christian name.) George was a friend and supporter of the Duke of Marlborough, who was godfather to Denver's eldest son, born in 1703 and christened Thomas George Churchill.

We have an intimate account of Thomas, the 10th Duke, and his son George Augustus, Viscount St. George, in letters and memoirs published as *Papers relating to the Family of Wimsey*. Here the Duke appears as a scholarly nobleman, autocratic and ill-tempered. On the other hand, St. George is represented as almost illiterate, but a man of principle and socially acceptable. There is an appraisal of them in a letter written in 1749 by Lord Chesterfield to his son, then in Rome:

> ... Your account of Lord S ... G ... does not altogether surprise me. I believe his defect to be, not any want of natural ability, but a wilfulness of disposition, which we may understand while we cannot but regret it. The Duke of D ... is a man of parts and education, who has studied everything in the ancient philosophers except the application of their precepts to himself. He will cite, very correctly, whatever Syrus says of the golden mean, or the Stoics, of self-government; yet all he does is dictated by passion and pursued to the point of extravagance. This makes him unjust, not indeed in his principles but certainly in his actions. His son, I dare say, finding that a man may be illiberal in spite of much learning, is determined to avoid the learning at any rate. He is thus sure of not resembling his father; but whether he has begun at the right end, your own good sense will judge. ...
>
> Nevertheless, I would have you cultivate Lord S ... G ..., for you have as much to learn from him

Thomas, tenth Duke of Denver

as he from you. You call him eminently illiterate, yet
you see that he is everywhere well received, for his
genteel figure and unaffected easy address. Such graces
are always captivating, not to women only but to
men. . . . Politeness without learning will pass better
than learning without politeness; but the best is, to
have both together; take care then to imitate only
what is admirable in these two men, and you will
become perfectly accomplished.

In 1751 Lord St. George astonished his friends and
enraged his father by marrying 'Bess' (surname not on
record), the widow of a hosier in Cheapside. She was
already his mistress, and willing to remain so, but she had
become 'so dear a Companion' that St. George insisted
on making her his wife. The affair was a nine days'
wonder. There were those (the Princess of Wales among
them) who thought he had acted as an honest man and
were prepared to receive his wife. Others could not
understand why he had gone to the lengths of marrying.
The Duke refused to see his son or to give him financial
support, and St. George and his wife, with a daughter
born shortly after their marriage, were reduced to living
in poor lodgings on 'a loan upon the postobits' (i.e.
repayable after the Duke's death), and the chancy
assistance of friends.

The Duke told an intermediary, who tried to reconcile
him and his son, that 'he had no objection, save a moral
one, to bastards; but for a young man to marry three
weeks before the birth, and thus legitimize what was

unlawfully begotten, was to make himself a laughing-stock. And after all, said he, the child turned out to be nothing but a daughter.'

At last St. George's elder sister, Lady Henrietta, unknown to their father, sent him sufficient money to leave London for France, where the Viscount thought to support himself by taking military service under the French king. In this project he hoped to have the assistance of his kinsman Christian Wimsey, a Major in Colonel Dillon's Regiment in Paris. Major Wimsey was the son of Mr. Richard Wimsey, the Duke's first cousin (though many years his senior) and successor to the titles if St. George should die. When old Mr. Richard heard of St. George's plan he wrote to Major Wimsey:

. . . I do most earnestly beg thou wilt dissuade him, by all means, from this hare-brained Enterprize. Do not, at any rate, be forward to assist him to a Commission in His Majesty of France's service. Consider what an Appearance it wd. have didst thou march him away to the Wars and he come to be killed there, on purpose (as it wd. seem) that thou and I should step over his dead Body into his Inheritance! . . . It wd. be the common talk that thou wast no better than thy poor Cousin's Murtherer; and indeed I shd. scarce know what else to call thee. I need not remind thee of this; thou hast seen it well enough already—only do not be over-persuaded.

Richard Wimsey's fears were justified. The Duke

called on him at his house near Romford (where he lived in retirement among his orchards and flower gardens), and openly accused him and Major Wimsey of a conspiracy to have St. George killed. Then followed an interview in which the Duke had the unusual and salutary experience of having the truth told him to his face. Richard, an older man and unimpressed by his rank, showed the Duke a letter from Major Wimsey making it clear that he had refused to help St. George to enter the French king's service. In an account of the interview he sent to his son, Richard Wimsey wrote:

You see, Cousin, said I, if your Son has applied to mine for his Interest, it is not with the Knowledge or Goodwill of either of us; but to speak plainly, I think it is not suitable to the Reputation of our Family that you shd. let yr. Dirty Linen be thus Wash'd in Publick, and, since the Marriage may not be Mended I recommend that you make the best of it, rather than let our Name become a Laughing-Stock. You are very free, said he, with your 'Cousin'. I told him, I wd. speak of his Grace when he showed me that he had any, and that he shd. use better Manners with a Kinsman so much older than himself. . . .

I beg you will at once acquaint our young Cousin with this Conversation, saying, I believe his Father to be sensible to the Dictates of Affection, if only he will not further Enrage him by foolish and unfilial behaviour.

The Duke vented his ill-temper on his wife and

daughters, until in desperation Lady Caroline wrote to her brother St. George describing a violent scene in which their father 'rav'd like a Madman' at the Duchess,

> . . . swearing that you had sucked in Poison with her Milk and that he believed you could be no son of his. I begged him not to speak so, for he would kill her. He said, He wished he could, 'and, Madam,' said he, 'as for that Puppy of yours, let him go and be killed in the Devil's name—shoot, hang or drown, all's one to me—and then I'll marry again and have an heir of my own getting.'

Caroline begged her brother to return if he would see his mother alive. Lord St. George returned in haste to England, and there followed a reconciliation which was the subject of as much gossip as the Viscount's marriage had caused. Fortunately for posterity, Horace Walpole mentioned it in a letter to Mr., afterwards Sir, Horace Mann:

> As for the Denver matter, it has all dwindled down. . . . The Duke brandished most Jovially his intention to marry again so soon as his Duchess should die; she, poor woman, appeared charitably to lend herself to this project; the daughters wept or lost at cards, each after her manner; and in the end, back post haste came Master Heir, as in Act V of any comedy you care to remember. The sisters smile again; the Duchess dismisses her pall-maker; the Duke gives a

mutter in Latin, kicks a footman downstairs, and there's an end. Only the wife, Lady St. George I mean, innocent of everything save being born nobody knows where, and married to nobody knows who, has been obliged to pay in kind for all these whimseys; elle s'est blessée; and thus our Duke, for all he knows, may by his fury have cheated himself out of an heir at second remove.

Walpole added that the Duchess 'has taken Lady St. George to her bosom and the infant to her knee; in short, she has at last something to be healthy for.' He also remarked that the Wimseys knew no half measures. 'With them it is god or clod, kiss or miss. And related to them, like the poor hack's pamphlet to the folio in calf, are strange ancient country personages through whose brains run the family mice.' As 'one such Meliboeus' he referred to Mr. Richard Wimsey,

. . . in a wig co-eval with Time, who adventured lately to Town as to the Indies, bringing his cousins a posy, and some brew much in use among the witches of his retreat as a solvent of melancholy. This Cousin Richard is he that must succeed, if the Viscount should die without issue, and I was informed he spoke with great earnestness of his distaste for the whole prospect; telling the Duke, besides, that he had now an obedient son, and might keep him so if he would resolve only to run mad, as hares do, once in a twelve-month. The Duke in his blue ribbon sat quiet under it all, and paid

this antique relic of Gothick simplicity the compliment
of d—ning him only after his departure; which was
undertaken upon a Rozinante, all four of whose legs
much blistering had stiffened, till they supported the
creature as those of a table do its top, where, if one but
fail, down comes all. However, there was no disaster
that I know; we may yet live to see Meliboeus and his
wig translated out of the Dorick style into the
Augustan, and, it may be, out of felicity into
uneasiness.

As the foregoing narrative shows the 10th Duke in a
somewhat unfavourable light, it seems advisable to
supplement it by quoting the epitaph on his tomb at
Duke's Denver, composed by the Revd. Micah Basing
who, as incumbent of the living from 1746 to 1773, was
in a position to estimate his patron's character.

Near this marble, in the vault of his Ancestors,
are deposited the earthly remains
of
The Right Noble
THOMAS GEORGE CHURCHILL WIMSEY
10th DUKE OF DENVER,
VISCOUNT ST. GEORGE AND
BARON WIMSEY
Knight of the Most Noble Order of the Garter
A new Ornament of an Ancient and Illustrious Family.
Animated by Attick Wit, Roman Vertue
and British Spirit,
and endued with solid understanding,
He was rich in mind no less than in substance,
Noble by nature as by birth,
And of his exalted Order the most fittingly entitled
HIS GRACE.

In his publick capacity, he served his Country
by example rather than by action,
Deeming it to be more suited to his great Station
To exhibit the abstract principles of Truth,
Justice and Honour,
than to become embroiled in the factions of
lesser men.

In his private life, he was devoted to
the interest of his Family,
A prudent director of his Household,
Condescending to those who enjoy'd his Patronage.

May the respectful Approbation
which his upright life gained for him from all orders
of men,
and the esteem in which he was held by his Sovereign,
be the prelude to
Applause from Angels,
and Acceptance by the King of Kings.

George, the 11th Duke, and 'Bess' had three children: the first-born daughter who lived to the age of sixty-five and remained single; William Stanhope, Viscount St. George, born in 1753 and eventually his father's successsor; and Lord Mortimer Wimsey, born in 1755, an eccentric recluse who became estranged from his family. Lord Mortimer's career, first outlined by Miss Sayers in her letter of 25 May 1936, quoted earlier, was narrated more fully in a pamphlet entitled:

An Account of LORD MORTIMER WIMSEY, The Hermit of the Wash, related in a Letter to Sir H—— G—— Bart.
by A Clergyman of the Church of England.
Bristol. Printed by M. Bryan, Corn-street; 1816.

The title-page also bears a quotation from the Revd. Jeremiah Tapp, D.D.: Commentary on Article XVII. The only clue to the identity of the writer is given by the initials T—— R—— at the end of the pamphlet. There are two baronets with the initials H. G. in the list in *Debrett's Peerage*, 1816, namely Sir Henry Goodricke, of Ribston, co. York, and Sir Henry Goring, of Shanecroy, co. Sussex.

The writer of the letter states that in 1810 he was staying with his friend, Dr. Jeremiah Tapp, vicar of Bittlesea in Norfolk, well known for his standard work, *Tapp on the Articles*. One morning after breakfast his host asked him whether he would care to accompany him to an outlying part of the parish known as Marsh Hallows, the vicar having some business there. 'And then', said he smiling, 'you may make the acquaintance of our local hermit.' They started out on ponies, and soon after leaving Bittlesea the road ceased and they proceeded by a series of droves across a land intersected by deep drains and dykes.

> At length we arrived at the place we were to visit; a group of mean little hovels, whose wretched inhabitants make their living by fishing and snaring wild-fowl in the fen. . . . When we had done what we came for, Dr Tapp informed me that we must now go forward on foot, if we were to carry out our design of visiting the hermit. . . . He then surprised me by saying that the poor Solitary who lived in this desolate retreat was a gentleman of noble birth, and indeed none other than the brother of the Duke of Denver, who is the owner of all this part of Norfolk, from Denver Sluice to the Wash. You may well conceive that my curiosity was greatly aroused, and that I was ready to undergo any exertions to obtain a sight of this remarkable figure. 'Remarkable indeed he is,' replied the worthy doctor, 'and so you will say when you see him.'

With the aid of a guide, and using poles to leap over water channels too wide to step across, they reached the sea-coast. There, beside a stream flowing into the Wash, they found a daub and wattle hut, not more than six feet high and ten feet long, with a door but no windows, a little protected from the sea by a wooden breakwater with a number of groynes. The hermit was not to be seen, but their guide, after gazing out to sea, gave several shrill halloos, like the cry of a sea bird, and after a time they saw a swimmer make his way up the estuary, draw himself out of the water and come stalking towards them.

'Now,' said Dr Tapp, 'you shall see him; but not hear him, for he speaks to nobody. And though he is by birth Lord Mortimer Wimsey, you must not call him so.' I asked, how then I ought to address him. Dr Tapp replied, 'The people about here are accustomed to call him old Scaley, but I speak to him by the name of Ichthus, which is the name he likes best.'

By this time this remarkable personage had approached and stood before us. He was entirely naked, except for a kind of girdle made of fish-skins which preserved the necessary minimum of modesty, and his skin was tanned to the brownness and hardness of leather by the action of the sun, wind and salt water. What added greatly to the oddity of his appearance was his hair, which hung to his shoulder-blades and was bleached a bright yellow. His aspect was the more pitiable, that he bore all the signs of having once been an exceedingly handsome man, his features being good, though harsh, and his eyes of a deep blue, with something very strange and melancholy in their expression. He bowed politely to us, with the air of one who had been brought up in the atmosphere of the court, and with a pleasant demeanour preceded us to the door of his dwelling which he opened and invited us by his gestures to enter. This we did, stooping our heads to pass through the low door. I observed that the hermit himself could not stand upright, except in the very centre of the hut. He lit a tallow candle from a little fire which smoked in one corner, and thus enabled us to examine our surroundings.

The place was very clean, but quite destitute of comfort or convenience, containing only a rough bed with woollen coverings, a chair and a table with a book open upon it. An iron pot, a pitcher and a wooden plate completed the furnishing of the abode.

My companion addressed the poor Solitary in a cheerful voice by the name of Ichthus, saying that we were come to pay him our respects, and had brought him some barley loaves to eat, such as were used for feeding the carp in the fish-pond at Bittlesea parsonage, 'for you know,' he went on, turning to me, 'Ichthus is one of those fish brought up by St. Peter in the Miraculous Draught, and therefore must eat nothing but such food as is suitable for fishes.' To this the strange being bowed his assent, and receiving the loaves which Dr Tapp took out of his wallet, seemed by his manner to express his gratitude for this attention. He then took up the book which lay on the table, and which I had perceived to be a volume of the Holy Scriptures, and presented it to me, making signs that I should read him some of it. Accordingly I read to him from the last chapter of St. John's Gospel, to which he listened with very becoming demeanour, nodding his head at mention of the catch of fishes and pointing to his own breast, as who should say, 'There was I.' After this, drawing out my own Bible and a lead-pencil from my pocket, I asked him whether he would write his name upon a blank leaf, as a memento of our visit. He smiled upon me and, taking the pencil, drew very neatly the outline of a fish, and beneath it in Greek letters the word *IXΘYΣ* which acrostically expresses Our Lord.

They took their leave of the hermit, and on their way home Dr. Tapp told his companion that Lord Mortimer Wimsey had been a youth of great promise but as an undergraduate at Cambridge he had been exposed to Evangelical and even Calvinistic influences, and had conceived the idea that he was foredoomed to utter damnation. For fifteen years he lived in a state of quiet but immovable despair, alternating with fits of religious horror. Then one morning when he was about thirty-six years of age,

. . . he came out of his chamber with so joyful a countenance as to astonish all those about him. He informed them that a revelation had been vouchsafed to him in the night; that he had found himself being drawn up in a great net out of the sea, together with a multitude of fishes, and had heard a voice saying, 'Mine own will I bring again, as I did sometime from the deep of the sea.' He had at once sought permission of his father to retire to this solitary spot and there remain till it should please the Lord to draw him home. Seeing that nothing else would content him, the Duke (though much against his own inclination) had permitted him to follow out this fancy of a disordered mind. Since coming to Marsh Hallows, some sixteen years before, he had spoken to no one, worn no clothes but the fish-skins we had seen upon him, and lived without any sustenance but such as a fish might be supposed to take, namely shrimps and shell-fish, and a kind of seaweed which he gathered from the groynes, together with fresh water from the stream and a few gifts of bread and corn brought to him from time to time by the cottagers.

The writer went on to say that he heard no more of the unfortunate gentleman until June 1815 when, being at Lowestoft, he observed a commotion in the town and was told it was the funeral of Lord Mortimer Wimsey, whose body had been recovered from the sea after several days immersion, in the nets of one of the trawlers. He attended the service, and afterwards took pains to discover the circumstances of the hermit's death. Three boys, returning from a night's fishing,

. . . perceived the Solitary standing and gazing with great earnestness towards the rising sun. As they came abreast of him, he called out eagerly to them, 'Have you seen Him? Have you seen Him?' At first they were so much astounded to hear Old Scaley (as they called him) speak, after a silence of over twenty years, that they scarcely knew how to answer; but when they had collected their wits they answered that they had seen nobody. 'But,' said he, 'can you not now see our Lord Himself, walking upon the water?' They looked in the direction to which he pointed but could see nothing except the dazzling brightness of the sun, which indeed threw a golden track across the waters of the North Sea, almost to where they stood. Then the Solitary cried out in a loud but melodious voice, 'Thou shalt open my lips, O Lord! The tongue of the dumb shall sing,' and at once casting himself into the sea began to swim very vigorously along the golden path of light towards the sunrise. They watched him for a considerable time, until he could no longer be seen, and then went home to tell their families of this remarkable occurrence.

About a week later the trawlers brought the body of Lord Mortimer to Lowestoft. One of the owners told the letter-writer,

. . . that as they were taking up their nets they found one of them to be very heavy and, calling on the next boat to assist them, they got it up with great difficulty, when it proved to contain a man's naked body, together with an astonishing multitude of fish, *so that their net brake.* Thus one may say that Lord Mortimer's vision was fulfilled in a truly wonderful manner. The dead man was easily recognised, not only by his stature and the colour of his hair, but also by his features, for although the corpse had been for some days in the water, it was singularly little disfigured. It was observed with some surprise that no member of the family attended the funeral; but the parents of the unfortunate gentleman being both dead, his brother and sister had never displayed any natural solicitude for his welfare, and it is supposed that they were ashamed of his eccentricity. The arrangements were therefore left in the hands of the incumbent of St. Margaret's Church, Lowestoft, and of the Revd. Dr Tapp, who caused him to be put in the coffin naked as he was found, with, for his sole shroud, the fishing net in which he was taken up. Subsequently a marble stone was placed over his grave, at the worthy Doctor's expense, bearing neither name nor title, but only the word *ΙΧΘΥΣ* and the verse of Scriptures (viz. Ps. LXVIII:22) which had been revealed to him in his vision.

When Miss Sayers first outlined the story of Lord Mortimer in a letter to me, she said that he was buried in a churchyard later undermined by the tides, so that 'the sea had him in the end'. However, the pamphlet states that the funeral arrangements were made by the incumbent of St. Margaret's, Lowestoft. Here the churchyard has not been subject to erosion. It is possible that while the incumbent of St. Margaret's made the arrangements, the service and burial took place at Pakefield, where the church stands on the cliff's edge. The tombstone provided by Dr. Tapp is not now to be found.

V

THE DENVERS OF THE
SECOND CREATION

A FEW DAYS after Lord Mortimer's burial his sister died, and William, the 12th Duke, married but childless, was left without near relatives. His heir was now a fourth cousin, Colonel George Wimsey, son of Thomas and only grandson of Major Christian Wimsey. Colonel Wimsey had been on Lord Wellington's staff in the Peninsular War, and was now with the newly-made Duke in Brussels. Denver wrote to Colonel Wimsey informing him of Mortimer's death, and inviting him to stay at Bredon Hall when his military duties should permit. Before a reply could be received, Denver learned that a great battle had been fought at a place called Waterloo. A few days later he had a letter from the Duke of Wellington telling him that Colonel Wimsey had been severely wounded in the battle, and, despite all that medical care could do, he had since died. Wellington expressed great regret at the loss of a brother officer so close to him as to rank as a personal friend, and his sympathy for Denver at being deprived of an heir to his honours.

Colonel Wimsey left an only daughter, Grace, who,

with her widowed mother, now made Bredon Hall their
home at the Duke's earnest request. Denver now faced
the future of the family with some dismay. At his death
the barony of Wimsey, descending to the heirs general,
would fall into abeyance between the lines sprung from
his two aunts, Henrietta and Caroline. The dukedom,
the earldom and the viscounty would become extinct
because these peerages passed down in the male line, and
Grace Wimsey could not inherit or transmit them.

There was one flourishing branch of the Wimsey
family, though not in the line of succession to the titles.
This was descended from Colonel John Wimsey, the
Parliamentarian, who married the 6th Duke's daughter
Elizabeth. Among these Wimseys the Christian name
Bredon occurred in most generations, perhaps an
indication that the collateral branch valued and wished
to show their kinship with the family at Bredon Hall.
They had prospered on their own account, and now had
estates in Norfolk and Leicestershire, and some property
on the Lincolnshire coast in the vicinity of Grimsby, and
likely to become valuable as that ancient port was
modernized and developed. The 12th Duke had a high
regard for his kinsman Sir Bredon Wimsey, and there
was no one he would rather contemplate as his successor
at Bredon Hall.

At Denver's invitation, Sir Bredon spent some weeks
at the Hall to discuss arrangements for the transfer of the
property, at the Duke's death, to Bredon and his heirs.
He was accompanied by his eldest son Charles, who was
naturally closely concerned. Charles and Grace Wimsey

became interested in the management of the estates and the household, and eventually (as perhaps their elders hoped) in one another. In due course a marriage was arranged between the future heir to Bredon Hall and the daughter of the last heir to the family honours.

Charles and Grace were married early in 1817, and the Duke now sounded his fellow peers about a special remainder enabling his titles to pass to Grace's descendants in the male line. This had the influential support of the Duke of Wellington, conscious that Denver's lack of a male heir was a consequence of Waterloo. It would probably have been allowed, but before a decision was reached Denver died, his barony became abeyant, and his higher titles extinct. Nevertheless, Wellington, with some other peers of high rank, made representations to the Crown that an historic dukedom should not be allowed to disappear, and in 1820 Charles Wimsey was created Duke of Denver and Viscount St. George. Technically he was the 1st Duke of the second creation, but as this was still in the Wimsey family he was usually styled the 13th Duke. Charles and Grace named their eldest son George Bredon after his two Wimsey grandfathers.

Notwithstanding the vicissitudes of the family, the Denvers of the second creation were fully representative of the earlier line. Four Dukes—the 9th to the 12th— were antecessors rather than ancestors, but George Bredon was descended through his mother from the whole ennobled line from the 1st Baron to the 8th Duke, and through his father from the ancient barons down to the 6th Duke as well as from the collateral branch.

George Bredon, who became the 14th Duke, married Mary Death—the second Wimsey–Death union, and the one which resulted in Lord Peter being named Death, and his sister, Mary. The eldest son of this marriage was christened Mortimer Gerald Bredon, the name Mortimer indicating that 'the Hermit of the Wash', forty years after his death, had become a commemorable figure in the Wimsey family.

Mortimer Gerald, the 15th Duke, married Honoria Lucasta, daughter of Francis Delagardie, of Bellingham Manor, Hampshire—the Dowager Duchess when Miss Sayers began her series of books. Duke Mortimer broke his neck in the hunting field in 1911, leaving Gerald Christian, who succeeded him, Lord Peter Death Bredon Wimsey and Lady Mary Wimsey.

Gerald Christian, the 16th Duke, married his cousin Helen, and they had a son Gerald ('Jerry'), styled Viscount St. George, and a daughter, Lady Winifred Wimsey. The only reference to her is in a letter on 'The Wimsey Chin', signed by 'Matthew Wimsey, p.p. Dorothy L. Sayers', published in *The Times*, 4 December 1937.

Lady Mary Wimsey married Chief Inspector Charles Parker, of the Criminal Investigation Department, Scotland Yard, and they had a son and a daughter.

Lord Peter Wimsey married, on 8 October 1935, Harriet Deborah Vane, only daughter of the late Henry Vane, M.D., of Great Pagford, Hertfordshire. Harriet

Vane's great-grandfather was an admiral, and had obtained a grant of armorial bearings. These were:

Arms: Azure, a weather-cock gold, in chief five estoiles archwise silver.

Crest: On a torse gold and azure, an anchor silver cabled gold, entwined by a wreath of laurel vert.

Motto: NEC SPE NEC GLORIA VANA.

Lord Peter had property of his own, having been left a piece of land on the outskirts of London. This, originally of trifling importance, became very valuable in the 1920s, and Lord Peter,

finding that it was falling into the hands of the speculative builder, suddenly developed a conscience about it and took things into his own hands, so that he is now the landlord as well as the ground-landlord of practically the whole of his own estate. This is profitable, as well as a good thing for the inhabitants, since he insists on a reasonable standard of efficiency and comeliness in such buildings as are put up on his property. His pubs are the object of his special consideration, and the publicans have to mind their p's and q's, since the landlord has a way of dropping in from time to time to sample the beer or throw a dart with the customers. As for his passage-of-arms with the Peculiar People, who wanted to erect a chapel of exceptionally hideous construction just opposite a particularly nice little block of experimental model

The Arms of Lord Peter Wimsey

houses put up by his own architect—that has become local history.

—D.L.S., in a letter dated 15 April 1936.

Lord and Lady Peter had three sons, whose names are given in 'Talboys' (1942) as Bredon, aged six; Roger, four; and Paul, the youngest. However, in a letter dated 12 November 1939 (*Spectator*, 17 November 1939), the Dowager Duchess refers to her then two grandsons as Bredon, just three, and Paul, nearly a year old. I cannot explain why she calls the second one Paul instead of Roger, unless it be that she was momentarily confused by a premonition that there would be another grandson of that name.

In this letter, written to an American friend, the Dowager Duchess gave an account of the family in the early days of the Second World War. Lord Peter had 'gone back to his old job, and everything comes without

The Arms of Harriet Vane

any proper address through the Foreign Office'. Lady Peter was at Tallboys with her two sons and the Parker children. St. George was in the Royal Air Force, and in December shot down a German bomber. Denver was worried about him, and the Dowager Duchess wrote to her friend:

His father says he ought to have got married to somebody first, so as to provide an heir in case of accidents. 'Really, Gerald,' I said, 'fancy worrying about that at a time like this. If there's anything left to be heir to when we've finished paying for the War, Peter's got two boys—and, judging by Jerry's present taste in young women, we are mercifully spared.' That was rather tactless, I suppose, because Gerald's fretting quite enough about the estate already; he says we shall be ruined, of course, but he doesn't mind that if only he can do his duty by the land.

Denver's concern for the estate is also reflected in an extract from the private diary of Lord Peter Wimsey, 'somewhere abroad' (*Spectator*, 8 December 1939).

. . . My brother writes that he is planting oak-trees in the Long Coppice. I acknowledge that there is something in him that is indomitable. He is persuaded that the next generation, if not this, will see the end of our stewardship, and for him (being what he is) that means the end of everything that was England. Even if we, by some miracle, are not left ruined beyond repair, even if a new kind of society does not take the soil from us and hand it over to God knows what kind of commercial spoliation, his personal situation is hopeless because he can place no confidence in his heir. He knows well enough Jerry would not care if the whole place were surrendered to ribbon-building or ragwort. But what the land requires the land shall have, so long as he is alive to serve it. All the same—oaks!

Lord Peter was on the point of setting out on a mission which would presumably take him into enemy territory. A week after the above entry he wrote in his diary:

. . . My papers have arrived, so the balloon goes up tonight. When M—— handed them over he said, 'You have a wife and family, haven't you?' I said 'Yes', and felt curiously self-conscious. The first time it has mattered a curse whether I went west or not. M——

looked at me as I used to look at my own married
officers when they volunteered for a dirty bit of work,
and it all seemed absurd and incongruous.

I shall not keep a diary *over there*. So in case of
accident, I will write my own epitaph now: HERE LIES
AN ANACHRONISM IN THE VAGUE EXPECTATION OF
ETERNITY.

We do not know what the mission was, or where it
took him, but in the summer of 1942 Peter and Harriet
were living at Tallboys, now with a third son. This we
find in the story entitled 'Talboys' (so spelt by the
American publisher), where there is a reference to Peter's
views on the responsibility of inherited property.
Harriet, discussing her three sons with Miss Quirk, a
visitor, mentions that Bredon had a particular position as
the eldest, and that 'the day is bound to come when they
realize that all Peter's real property is entailed.'

Miss Quirk said that she so much preferred the French
custom of dividing all the property equally. 'It's so
much better for the children.'

'Yes, but it's very bad for the property.'

'But Peter wouldn't put his property before his
children!'

Harriet smiled.

'My dear Miss Quirk! Peter's fifty-two, and he's
reverting to type.'

This suggests that Lord Peter shared his brother's sense

of duty towards the estates, and that he would be as careful a steward if ever he inherited the Denver property.

With 'Talboys' the written canon came to an end, but Miss Sayers told me, and some others, that she did not expect 'Jerry' to survive the war. There is no record of his death, but I think we may believe that Viscount St. George gave his life for his country, and is more honoured than if he had lived to be the Duke of Denver who let his land go to 'ribbon-building or ragwort'.

Accordingly Lord Peter became heir presumptive to the dukedom, with Bredon next in line of succession. The Wimsey canon takes us no further, but whatever the name of the present Duke the family goes on, and though its historian be told that it is unknown at the Palace of Westminster or the Heralds' College, I HOLD BY MY WHIMSY.